How to Survive a Job You Hate

Joseph Gilar

© 2019, Joseph M. Gilar. All rights reserved. No part of this publication may be reproduced, stored in a retrieval system, or transmitted in any form or by any means without the prior written permission of the author.

ISBN: 9781795319300

Table of Contents

Introduction 1
Chapter One: When to Work 5
Chapter Two: Do More of What You Like and Less of What You Don't Like ... 10
Chapter Three: Create an Impression of Productivity 12
Chapter Four: Be a Team Player 15
Chapter Five: Miscellaneous Strategies 18
Chapter Six: If Firing is Imminent 21
Chapter Seven: Conclusions 24
About the Author 25

v

Introduction

How to Survive a Job You Hate is a practical guide to increased job satisfaction. This book will help improve your time at work—whether you don't like your coworkers, the work itself, or both. It includes advice on how you can be viewed as a highly productive employee, a goal not always easy to attain when you have little or no interest in your work. Suggestions in *How to Survive a Job You Hate* will be useful even for those who like their jobs. But this book was written primarily for unhappy employees.

Chapter One discusses how to use whatever control you have over your work time to your advantage. Chapter Two addresses arranging your job to do more of what you prefer—which can be tasks you like or those you dislike less. Chapter Three presents tips to convey the impression that you're more productive than you actually are. Chapter Four considers how to be regarded as a team player, a perception that can only help you. Chapter Five contains miscellaneous strategies that can be useful in certain work environments. Chapter Six covers a situation when being fired is imminent—and how to delay and possibly reverse what appears to be an inevitable termination.

How to Survive a Job You Hate is different from other books with similar titles. Many books written to help people who are unhappy at work advise switching careers, networking to find better jobs, creating more compelling resumes, starting businesses or otherwise becoming entrepreneurial, and retraining to acquire new skills by taking courses during evenings/weekends or self-study. But these typically are not short-term solutions. They don't help with the job you have to go to today, tomorrow, and next week.

Then there is psychological advice on handling stress, dealing with difficult people, and expressing gratitude for and emphasizing the positive elements of your job—the pay, if nothing else. Plus ideas on healthy lifestyles—diet, exercise, meditation, and the like—that can improve any situation, not just work.

And then there are entertaining stories illustrating that you're not the only one with a boss from hell or weird coworkers.

All this is well and good. But what's not covered in other books are practical ideas for people who dread the job they have *now*. Of course you don't have to absolutely *hate* your job. You just don't look forward to going to work. Maybe it's boring. Or stressful. Or you don't like your supervisor or some of your coworkers. Or there are plenty of other things you'd rather be doing. *How to Survive a Job You Hate* is designed for all these situations.

Many people are stuck in their jobs. Employees near retirement may need steady pay for just a few more years and do not have the longer time horizon that would make retraining—or even job searching—worthwhile. Residents of sparsely populated areas may face limited job alternatives without moving, and many factors—for urban and suburban as well as rural dwellers—can make a move impractical: kids in schools they like, proximity to aging relatives who need assistance, a weak housing market in which homeowners can't sell their home at an attractive price, or a convenient commute to an otherwise unappealing job. In any case, while pursuing or not pursuing work alternatives or a healthier lifestyle, right now you may be in a job you dislike. And you're there because you need the pay and there's no obvious alternative at the moment. So the focus of this book is not finding new work or improving your psychology or developing a healthier lifestyle but instead practical strategies on *How to Survive a Job You Hate*.

The discussion throughout assumes a job in an office in the United States in a work group with at least a boss and a couple of coworkers. It may be a small business or a large corporation. Suggestions for the office scenario can be applied to other situations but, frankly, office work allows many strategies that are not always available in environments where workers can be closely monitored—such as construction sites. Also, although some discussion, especially about holidays, applies directly to work in the United States, it should be straightforward to modify the basic points for jobs located elsewhere.

But before getting into these strategies, a healthy dose of reality is essential. Assess as objectively as possible how good or bad your job really is. How does it compare with past or possible future jobs? Rate some of the following (or other characteristics you feel are pertinent): your commute, work content, manager, coworkers, pay, benefits, and hours of work including evening and weekends that affect your work-life balance. Perhaps grade each item one to ten and then sum the grades to see how many points your job scores out of the maximum possible. If there are eight items rated one to ten, the maximum total would be 80. But equal weighting is not mandatory. Essential criteria can be given more weight than minor features. The quality of the on-site cafeteria might get a maximum of two points, the commute three points, but the fit of the job duties to your skill set ten points. Compare your present job with those you've held in the past or future possibilities—using the bottom-line sum as well as the line-by-line ratings for each characteristic you list.

You can experiment with different sets of job criteria and maximum ratings. A striking outcome of an exercise like this is when you prefer job A to job B but B gets a higher score than A. These "reversals" might induce you to re-evaluate your criteria's maximum scores as well as their individual ratings or to add additional job attributes. Most important, don't be quick to assume that a relatively unknown job elsewhere—or, even more so, hypothetical job prospects—will be better.

Here's an example: Emily is a third-year associate at a high-powered private law firm. Her work is engaging and she's well-paid, but she works a stressful 60 hours per week. If she stays there four or five more years she'll be considered for partner. Partnership at her law firm would at least triple her present salary. But there are about five associates for each future partner slot so Emily's chance to achieve partner is about one in five or 20 percent. If Emily doesn't make partner, she would probably receive job offers from clients of her firm with a salary roughly equal to what she earns now.

Recently Emily was offered a position as an attorney for her county government. The work would be easier with fewer hours than at the law firm. But Emily's salary would be about two-thirds of her present pay with no promise of the level of compensation partners in private law firms achieve. The county office is walking distance from her apartment, while the law firm is a 30-minute drive away. Below are Emily's ratings:

Job Characteristic	Maximum Score	Law Firm	County Gov't
Pay: present and future	10	10	4
Work-life balance	10	3	10
Interest in the work	8	7	4
Commute	5	2	5
Total Score	33	22	23

The county job "wins" here 23-22, but the score is very close. Emily was skeptical. Maybe the result was close because her 10 rating for law firm pay assumed she'd make partner when there's only a 20 percent chance of that happening. In any event, this exercise led Emily to consider more alternatives including working for a client company that would like to hire her but has been assuming she wants to stay at her law firm to have a chance to make partner. In many ways the client firm would be intermediate between her present job and the county offer. So Emily went back to the drawing board with three alternatives rather than two:

Job Characteristic	Max Score	Law Firm	County Gov't	Client
Pay: present and future	10	10	4	7
Work-life balance	10	3	10	8
Interest in the work	8	7	4	6
Commute	5	2	5	3
Total Score	33	22	23	24

Although this exercise produced only a narrow "victory" for the client company, Emily's reaction was a big smile and an out-loud "Yes!" Her response—and not the mere numbers—revealed her gut feeling. Upon further thought, Emily realized she liked the people at the client company more than those at the law firm (she didn't know anyone at the county well)—a significant criterion she had omitted from her list. So it's not the numbers alone—interpreting the result is crucial.

But no matter the score for your present job, let's examine how to improve it!

Chapter One: When to Work

This may seem a strange topic. Don't jobs have set hours—something like 8:30 to 5:00, Monday through Friday? How can an employee choose when to work?

Well, you have more flexibility than you may think. You usually can choose your vacation days, what times you go to lunch or take breaks, and when to schedule visits to doctors and dentists—for yourself or family members. You can almost always go to the restroom whenever you like. Maybe you can sometimes—or often—work from home. And there may be "flex time" where you can work four ten-hour days rather than five eight-hour days each week, or 7 AM to 3:30 PM instead of 9 AM to 5:30 PM. The basic idea is, to the extent possible, work when your boss and obnoxious coworkers are off, and take off when they're likely to work. In that way you can reduce the amount of time you're spending around people you'd rather not be with. Possibly this strategy may also help you avoid hectic work days and let you work at times when the office workload is lighter.

Let's start with paid time off, often something like two weeks for those with no more than three years on the job, then three weeks in years four and five, and, finally, four weeks for those who've put in at least five full years. It may be possible to buy additional vacation time by taking a week or more off without pay—but that's not an attractive option when you need the money.

Many employees take off all day or leave early on days right before holidays. These days sometimes have formal early dismissals. With fewer people around and less work, those coming to the office are likely to have an easy day.

The best days to work include:

- The last week of the calendar year because many people take off between Christmas and New Year's so there's likely a reduced work load as well as fewer coworkers around. Some take off this week because they failed to plan vacations earlier in the year and face "use or lose" paid time off. Don't be one of those!

- Days right before Christmas when there are holiday parties at the office
- Days immediately before holidays, especially those not generally celebrated on Mondays: the Fourth of July, Thanksgiving, Christmas, and New Year's Day. Some employers allow early pre-holiday dismissals on these days, and, when they don't, many workers take time off anyway to get a jump on holiday traffic.
- Friday after Thanksgiving, a day when many people extend their Thanksgiving holiday (and which is becoming a standard holiday at some companies)
- Wednesday before Thanksgiving, a day many, especially those traveling, are off from work
- Days when there will be celebrations—retirement or birthday parties, fun outings, talks by the CEO or other high officials, or special programs that take you out of the office (such as a panel of executive vice-presidents discussing a future office reorganization)
- Days when coworkers you particularly dislike, perhaps including your manager, are taking off (in some offices those days are planned in advance and noted on group calendars)

The problem, of course, is that you may not want to work on some of the days listed above because that's when your friends and family are off from work or school. But working even some of those days will reduce contact with your coworkers—and thereby can make your work life more pleasant.

Now let's consider reshaping the work week. Many employers are sympathetic to flexible ("flex") time that allows people to start or end work earlier or later than most employees. Reducing peak-time commuting, pollution, and crowds all have environmental benefits that have encouraged flexible work schedules.

Suppose you can start and end work two hours earlier than others in your office. Then you're with them only six rather than eight hours per day. Those two hours with fewer people around may be the workday's best time. They can be your most productive hours if you're not then distracted by e-mails or scheduled meetings. Similar points hold for those who work late. I recall an acquaintance who convinced his employer that he could only fall asleep quite late at night and as a result slept through the morning. He managed to arrange his regular hours to be noon to 8 PM. Years later he confided that because everyone else typically left the office by 6 PM, he could go home well before 8 PM and had more like a 30-hour than a 40-hour work week.

Sometimes hours flexibility is readily granted. But in some environments flex time may be permitted only under special circumstances—such as you live further from the office than most or commute from a different direction or have family responsibilities that make getting home early more critical for you than for others. In case full flex time is not immediately allowed, you can at least from time to time mention your circumstances in the hope of achieving occasional flex time or increasing the chance that full flex time will ultimately be granted to you. Asking for odd times off may make your supervisor aware that flex time would particularly suit you—and supervisors will often provide such accommodation when it costs them little or nothing. Finally, talking to coworkers who have flex time may yield ideas on how you can convince your manager to allow it for you.

So far we've considered vacation days and hours during the day. You may also be able to reduce days per week. A popular federal government arrangement is to work nine-hour days Monday through Thursday and to alternate Fridays between eight hours and a full day off. This yields 80 hours every two-week pay period, eight days of nine hours for 72 of those 80 plus the alternate Friday for the other eight. This arrangement cuts days in the office—and commuting—by one out of ten or 10 percent. A few employees schedule four ten-hour days per week, which reduces days worked per week by one out of five or 20 percent.

Some employers have other categories of time off in addition to vacations. Sick leave is common and almost always includes doctor and dentist visits for yourself and those you care for, so these can be arranged during active work hours rather than, say, days right before holidays or (even worse!) weekends. Some employers offer two or three days of paid leave per year to take care of family or for appointments such as renewing a driver's license or closing on a new home. This is not to be confused with the *unpaid* leave of up to 12 weeks to care for a close relative under the Family and Medical Leave Act.

Another category is bereavement. Designed to allow attendance at funerals of close friends and relatives, this paid leave can be used even to go to funerals of neighbors or others you don't know very well—which may or may not be preferable to a full day of work. Whether to attend midday funerals that could require two round trips to work can be a tough decision for funerals of those other than relatives or close friends. No one in your office is likely to check the funeral details so you may be able to take a couple of hours off rather than returning to work.

And there's more. On work days you can take time off when others are working and be in the office while they're at lunch. Develop a reputation as someone who likes to eat lunch early (maybe because you skip breakfast) or late (perhaps because you eat big breakfasts). Then you can be out of the office for lunch while your coworkers are working and in the office while they're out. Whatever your timing, it can be very refreshing to change your environment during lunch, if possible, by walking or driving to another part of town or meeting a friend who doesn't work where you do. And just as you can go to lunch earlier or later than others, you can also take coffee breaks when others don't and remain in your immediate office environment when they're on break.

Even when you don't like most of your coworkers, there may be exceptions. So instead of taking lunch or breaks at odd times, you can take them at the usual times but with coworkers whose companionship you enjoy.

Leaving your primary workspace to go to another part of the building or campus in which you work is another way to avoid unpleasant coworkers. You may have occasion to go to a library, print center, or other facility. Visit those places during peak hours when you can avoid being around your coworkers rather than at lunchtime or early or late in the day when they're not around anyway.

With the shift towards open space rather than private offices (for all but the highest-level employees), hiding out in your office is an uncommon possibility but one that may still work for some. A locked office door suggests a meeting or a work-related phone call but can also provide an opportunity for anything from personal phone calls to on-line surfing to a nap.

One activity that no one can object to is going to the restroom. Even when you don't have to go, sitting in a private stall checking your phone, reading an article you printed out or tore off from a magazine or newspaper, or working on a puzzle you enjoy are possible activities. No one knows what you're doing in there. And stereotypes support repeated restroom visits for some: Many assume that older people, pregnant women, and those who appear to be in less than prime health need to visit restrooms more frequently than others.

We've saved the best for last: working at home whenever possible. Some people manage to work at home—*telecommute* is the technical term—all the time. You can't do a better job of avoiding the office and coworkers than by working at home. And there are so many other advantages—no commuting, dressing as you please, and multitasking household chores while working. On a conference call with your mute button on while others are speaking, you can be putting away dishes or sorting laundry. You may even be able to work from your favorite coffee shop or outside on nice days. But it can be difficult to work with spouses, kids, or pets at home, let alone strangers if you're working elsewhere. And if you're the typical employee with a laptop in your home office—or on your dedicated work table—you may feel you're never away from work. However, that laptop at home—whether it's there all the time or you carry it back and forth—can be a key to maintaining your job, as will be discussed more in Chapter Three.

In this chapter we've been talking about avoiding your coworkers and reducing your time in the office environment. These time shifts can involve a reduction in work effort because you're choosing to be in the office when it's not so busy and away when the work pace is heavy. (Alternatively, you may like working when fewer people are around when you can get more done.) In any event, if you reduce your work effort too much, eventually your manager will notice your lack of work and you'll get that "pink slip"—the old-fashioned American notice that you're fired. Well, not so fast—there are places where it's extremely difficult to get fired, perhaps the best example being the federal government where I have heard numerous anecdotes about people who've done little or no work for years—spending much of their work day surfing the web, reading material unrelated to the job, taking long lunch and other breaks, schmoozing with like-minded coworkers, even napping. There are other work environments where employees are well-protected from termination by unions or state or local regulations or honchos who like them or for whom they may be doing various *favors*—but let's not go there. In any event, these are rare situations. In almost all cases, to keep your job you need to produce—or at least give the impression that you're producing—especially when pursuing the aloof stance discussed in this chapter.

Chapter Two: Do More of What You Like and Less of What You Don't Like

If you like what you do at work but prefer not to be around your coworkers, Chapter One has covered much of what you need. (Chapter Four covers more interpersonal issues.) But if you dislike your work, whether you like your coworkers or not, then this chapter is for you. A safe assumption is that you don't want to be fired—and that you want to quit your present job only when you find a better situation—whether it's another job or time to devote yourself to family, volunteer work, or retirement. Many people seriously need the money they earn at their job and can't immediately find another job. So their dilemma is: They hate the work, but they must be productive—or at least give the impression they're productive—or else they'll lose their job and the money that comes with it.

So how do you get work done if the tasks are boring or difficult or otherwise unpleasant? And let's also assume you're not in one of those rare situations where you're related to the owner, your immediate boss, or another high-powered manager; not having an affair with someone influential (which is in many cases only a temporary situation); and not in an employee-protected environment like those described at the end of Chapter One where you can't get fired even if you screw around all day at work.

The short answer is: You're going to have to suck it up and work. The longer answer has three parts. First, most jobs require more than one type of work so try to arrange your job to do more of what you like (or dislike less) and not as much of what you don't like. Second, create the impression you're productive. Third, develop a reputation as likeable and a team player—which may be difficult to do if you don't like your coworkers, but is not impossible. Doing more of what you like and less of what you don't like is discussed in this chapter. The two other issues just mentioned are the topics of Chapters Three and Four.

Sue is a computer programmer looking forward to retirement. Technology is changing so fast that to keep up, Sue would need to learn new programming languages and techniques. But she's not motivated to improve her coding skills. It takes a while to learn new material and it's not worth it as much if you're near retirement as opposed to having decades more of work when you could use the new skills to increase your productivity—and pay.

But Sue's job is more than coding. She also writes reports summarizing her results. Sue is a better writer than most of her coworkers and, although she may not love technical writing, she likes writing better than programming. So Sue has an informal agreement with coworker Alex, a recent immigrant who is an excellent programmer but struggles to write reports in English, which is not his native language. Here's their arrangement: Alex reviews the work Sue has been assigned and suggests a few lines of efficient code that Sue can use as an outline for the rest of her program. In return, Sue reviews Alex's rough drafts, corrects his grammatical errors, and suggests edits.

The general point is to consider your full set of job duties. Even if you hate them all, you will like some more—or hate some less—than others. In Sue's case, the two duties are coding and writing. Sue worked things out with Alex so she does more writing and less coding. Both Sue and Alex gain from their informal agreement. In some cases, it may be a good idea for their team leader to be aware of their arrangement. Possibly their manager will decide that Sue should become the team editor and do no programming at all, a situation that would essentially give Sue a new and preferred job. But some managers are narrow-minded or have to be narrow-minded about job duties, especially in large organizations. So it may be better for Sue and Alex to keep their situation quiet and, by doing so, create the impression that Sue is a better coder than she is and Alex a better writer than he is.

Many jobs have more than two functions. Think about the types of work that make up your job. Can you rearrange your work to do more of what you like and less of what you don't like—either by a formal redefinition of your job or an informal arrangement like the one worked out by Sue and Alex? One possibility is to express enthusiasm about certain types of work—perhaps after a project is completed or during a performance review. Managers generally understand that people do better work when they like what they do—so letting your supervisor know what you like best may lead to your being assigned preferred job duties. Even better, emphasizing that you are especially productive completing certain tasks rather than that you like certain types of work can be the key to gaining assignments you like best—or, again, dislike least. There will not always be a cooperative coworker with complementary skills, like Alex, whose job duties you can informally share.

Chapter Three: Create an Impression of Productivity

Many people who dislike their jobs put forth minimal effort, dread group meetings, and display little or no passion about their work. This attitude is not conducive to maintaining a job, let alone being promoted. Lack of enthusiasm never helps and can lead to subpar performance ratings and maybe eventual termination even when your workplace is not reducing the overall number of employees.

But how can you do more than the minimum if you hate your work—and just want to fulfill your basic requirements and go home? There are at least five plans of action that take little effort and create an impression of high productivity:

- Attendance and punctuality. Make sure you never miss a meeting or an on-line or phone conference (unless, of course, you have a good reason to miss one, such as a higher-priority meeting). Print out or write down your schedule each day if you have to. Arrive a minute or so early, for example, 10:59 for an 11:00 meeting. Excellent attendance and punctuality is exactly what you *don't* expect from slackers and what you *do* expect from those who love their job. So this is one easy way to create an impression of productivity and competence. Similarly, promptly complete on-line courses, employee surveys, travel/expense reports, self- or other performance reviews, and various requested forms and documentation.
- Meetings. Pay close attention. Obviously, refrain from checking your phone, doodling, or similar distractions. Try hard to think of things you can say. This can be difficult to do for employees who dislike their

jobs, but being silent at all meetings suggests boredom—which may be the case, but you don't want to show it. Sometimes reviewing files, especially decks with slides, sent in advance that will be discussed at a meeting will trigger suggestions of what to say. Perhaps ask questions (even asking what an abbreviation stands for shows some curiosity—as long as it isn't an abbreviation everyone is expected to know, so check out the Internet—including your company's website—first). At the meeting point out a relationship between what's being presented and what was discussed at another time while noting that your point may be of general interest to your colleagues. Show enthusiasm for new ideas and proposals. When someone suggests a project or an alternative way of looking at an issue, join others' excitement—even if you really don't share it. Work will typically be assigned (or not) to you or your group no matter what you express, so avoid being the sourpuss among eager beavers! If it turns out there's flexibility in an assignment, you can later talk to your manager and explain that the new work sounded great for your team but doesn't quite fit your skill set. Suggesting other work you can do or pointing out your already full workload can be helpful in avoiding an unpleasant task.

- Reading material. You may discover on-line articles of relevance to your work unit, especially to your boss. Some of these may be emailed to you (although if sent to you, they likely also went to some, maybe all, of your immediate coworkers). You could search for articles on appropriate industry or competitor websites, and even summarize the material, but these suggestions may involve too much effort for a job you don't like. In any case, sending these sorts of emails will signal that you're an employee involved in your work and helpful to your colleagues.
- Extra work. Sometimes just a little additional work can help a great deal. Hector works for a clothing manufacturer and tracks the number of belts sold each month—by color and style. In addition to writing the standard monthly report, based on data collected within a spreadsheet, Hector could with little effort report additional results such as changes by month or since the same month last year, for example, the company sold 1.3% more black belts in October than September, and 3.5% more brown belts this January than last January. Analogously to sports teams' achievements, Hector may be able to report that a given month set a new sales record for a type of belt, perhaps in a store or a geographic area. With these simple additional calculations, Hector will be viewed as going above and beyond his basic duties. These extras may be boring but in many cases will be fairly easy to do, and they

suggest—and may eventually increase—job enthusiasm and productivity. Questions such as whether February's sales gain since last February exceeded the corresponding growth for January can become a little game that may make a job more enjoyable.
- Emails during off hours. Now and then send an email—especially when your boss or your boss' boss is one of the recipients—early in the morning before the standard work day, late in the evening, or on weekends or holidays. This is especially easy to do for those who work at home. Others will have to remember to take home their laptop—and use it! People are more likely to remember that you were working off hours than the content of your email. Working outside normal work hours is not something slackers do.

The basic idea here is: If you dislike your job, it will show up in one way or another—such as mediocre reports or a lack of engagement in one-on-one discussions or larger meetings. So you need counter strategies like those just described to offset a possibly poor impression you've been creating.

Chapter Four: Be a Team Player

Whatever your opinion of your boss and coworkers, inevitably there will be some people you like better than others. Try to spend more time with them. What's more important, try not to make enemies and, to the extent possible, be a likeable team player.

Let's take the simpler of these two issues first. Chapter One's advice about avoiding coworkers should be applied specifically to people you don't like. So, if you can't stand Jack but like Jill, tend to schedule your vacations when Jack is working and plan to be at work when Jill is also there. Even short chats with those you like—including people outside your department at security posts, the cafeteria, or the library—can make the day more pleasant. Within your team try to choose those you work with on group assignments. Be aware of future projects and volunteer to work with Jill—before you are assigned to work with Jack.

Allies at work are always an asset. It's not just being on good terms with coworkers to make the job environment more pleasant. Coworkers can also provide information on future developments that may help you ask for work you prefer and avoid work you like less. If your office has a hierarchy with detailed organization charts, it may be unusual for people to cultivate good relationships with those in lower-level jobs. But those employees may especially appreciate your attention that others at your level don't give them—and they can be very helpful allies. In addition, be ready to congratulate people on promotions, awards, and other work-related achievements as well as personal milestones such as getting married.

No matter what you do, most of your time with people at work will be spent with your manager and immediate coworkers. Whatever you think of them, it will be helpful if they consider you likeable and a team player. Here are eight ideas:

- Don't make enemies. Never say anything bad about a coworker even when discussing topics unrelated to work, and be very careful about saying negative things even about the work itself. If someone is criticizing another employee—whether the criticism is work-related or not, don't join in. Don't even smile on hearing such comments. Ideally, leave the conversation as soon as you can—without giving the impression that you're not a good listener: Respectful and attentive listening to your coworkers is a major plus. Definitely avoid political discussions. Although you may be in an environment where it seems everyone's opinions are the same, people's views tend to range across the political spectrum. Those with unpopular points of view may be keeping quiet. Any political comment is likely to appeal to some and offend others. And you'll lose more by offending one half than you'll gain by what will be considered an expected agreement with the other half. It should also be obvious that your job is the wrong place for discussions about religion, particularly if you are gung-ho on enlightening the unwashed. An exception is that any topic can be safe with a true friend, if you happen to develop such a relationship at work. (Avoiding making enemies doesn't mean you can never push back. But when you do push back, make it a work issue, not a personal issue. Example: James finished a deck of slides two weeks before a quarterly status meeting. The afternoon before that meeting Kevin asked him to add a couple of slides. To do so James had to stay at work until 8 PM. Whatever the reason for Kevin's delayed feedback, James has the right to complain to his manager. But James should make it a general issue of providing feedback well in advance of deadlines rather than a personal attack on Kevin.)

- Be aware of your coworkers' deadlines and give priority to those with the earliest deadlines working on the most pressing tasks. Make them look good by providing the input they need on time.
- Respect other people's needs. Suppose Jen sends you an email with a question while you are busy working on an unrelated matter that will take three hours to finish. Answer her email immediately. Your quick reply will show you take her concerns seriously, and your other work will be done in three hours and five minutes instead of three hours—an inconsequential difference that pales in contrast to how much Jen will appreciate your quick reply.
- The same point about a reply email holds for more complex tasks such as reviewing a draft. Here you may have to make a judgment call. If instead of just an email, coworker Brian sends you a draft to review that will take you an hour, you have a tradeoff to assess: Is reviewing Brian's draft better or worse for your job success than finishing other assignments earlier? The answer will vary. If your boss is traveling and won't be in until tomorrow, then go with Brian. On the other hand, if the project your manager assigned is required for a meeting later that

afternoon, work on that. But just as there's almost always time for a five-minute water-cooler or restroom break, there will be time to let Brian know you're sorry you can't get to his memo immediately but you'll do so right after your meeting. Showing respect will put you in a coworker's good graces.

- People contribute in ways other than work. Maybe you decorate rooms for office parties. Or bring in homemade cookies. Or you're a star on the company softball team. Or a responsible driver for a car pool that includes one or more coworkers. Sometimes you may have the opportunity to visit sick coworkers, attend funerals of their relatives, or help their parents or children with rides or household errands or repairs. These actions make you more likeable and give an impression of responsibility. Can't hurt.
- Think of ways you can help people on the job. A newbie will appreciate learning basic facts about the office—where are good places to park, when the snack bar is open, etc. Rare is the employee who couldn't benefit from improving one or more job skills—such as writing or using office software. You don't have to become a personal tutor. Sometimes sending a helpful link or a single comment will be much appreciated.
- Compliment people publicly—or to their manager privately—when praise is deserved, of course: Insincere expressions don't help anyone. In return, the complimented employee might be on the lookout to help you in some way—maybe with similar praise or providing valuable information.
- And the easiest one: Use mugs, mousepads, and other items with company logos. Wear t-shirts with the firm's name when appropriate. Look for other ways to identify with the company you work for—and indirectly with your work team.

These recommendations focus on improving your relationships with coworkers but not with your boss—the one who really counts. But in a world of 360 performance reviews where people above, below, and at your job level evaluate your work, it helps to be on good terms and be appreciated by everyone. And give managers credit: They can tell who is contributing and who isn't.

Chapter Five: Miscellaneous Strategies

The discussion so far covers strategies that can help most workers. In addition, there are occasional situations in which developing unusual game plans can improve your work life.

Most—but not all—employees are paid according to how much time they spend at work. But independent lawyers, consultants, therapists, and others are often paid only for billable hours, not for time at the office. Workers in other occupations are paid commissions based on sales or other results. Telephone salespeople can be paid by the hour or by the number of callers closed, that is, those who buy the company's product. Then there are intermediate situations where you are paid by time worked but evaluated periodically by how many sales you produce or how many customers you serve.

In any case, if you are paid purely by the hour, then you may welcome circumstances that are inefficient from your employer's viewpoint. Kim is a customer service rep spending most of her workday on the phone. Some callers paying by credit card need to search for either their card left in a wallet in another room or an account number on an invoice. Down times like these are welcome breaks for Kim. She can relax and check her personal phone or simply daydream. Even better are calls with conversations that develop into relaxing chit-chat unrelated to the product Kim's company is selling and servicing. Short breaks from work-related conversations can improve the workday. Unfortunately, the increasing trend of recording phone calls later reviewed by management interferes with this tactic.

Contractors and consultants obviously have a great deal of contact with clients. All the comments above about getting along with coworkers apply even more so with clients. You don't want your client reporting a problem to your employer. It may be especially helpful to develop a very good relationship with at least one person at a site to which you are assigned or visit regularly. Administrative assistants can be especially valuable contacts and are sometimes not given full respect by others, particularly higher-paid people within or outside their firm.

Here are two examples of how an administrative assistant can be supportive: First, suppose you do something careless such as leaving your keys at a client site. It could be very embarrassing to ask your primary client contact about your keys—for one thing, it suggests a lack of responsibility that the client would like to think is part of the service you're providing. In contrast, the admin may not only keep your loss of keys between the two of you so as not to embarrass you to others but may also be the best source of information for your client's lost-and-found procedures including where found items are returned. Second, suppose you need something from the client but the client has not responded. It may be a report you need to complete your assignment or pay for past work. Asking the admin for help here can be most valuable. No one wants to appear irresponsible or cheap to their own admin so the admin asking on your behalf can produce quicker results than your repeated efforts.

In our increasingly complex world, supervisors are not always aware how long work will take. They may not know how much time is involved in obtaining the necessary raw information—from the Internet, other departments, or archived files. And they may not understand how much work it is to transform this raw information into the required reports. For instance, many supervisors are not up to date on the latest data analysis tools used by those reporting to them. But you know your own work. So suppose at 1 PM your supervisor gives you a task to be completed by 4:30. You know it will take you only an hour. But don't reveal this. Instead, complete the work at a leisurely pace by 3:30, impress your supervisor by having the final product ready an hour early, and spend the other one and a half hours between 1:00 and 3:30 doing something you'd rather be doing.

A related point is when to send emails indicating you've completed a project. In the scenario just discussed, suppose those who assigned it have an hour meeting beginning at 3:30. If you send them an email with your completed work as an attachment at 3:15, one of them may be able to look at it quickly and give you something else to do. But if you send the same email at 3:45, they won't get to it until the meeting is over, at 4:30, when you're less likely to get additional work that's expected to be done that afternoon. And you'll still get credit for completing your work early. If you use this technique often, be sure to send emails at odd times such as 3:43 or 3:46. Too many emails sent right on the quarter-hour or half-hour, or even worse, right at the top of the hour, may seem contrived. And review those emails before hitting the send button—using your clearest writing, correct grammar, and no misspellings! (That's not strictly a job survival tool, but a point that can't be emphasized enough!)

Job sharing is an occasional option. To return, to our Chapter Two example, Sue has two job duties: coding and writing. Suppose her writing skills are recognized by another department that sometimes needs help editing reports. If Sue can arrange a job-sharing arrangement to work in both departments, she may be somewhat overworked but she could have possibilities of free time during the work day. When Sue is not around, her manager in one department will assume Sue is working in the other one. But Sue could be spending time leisurely walking from one department to the other, taking a coffee break, or chatting with people. These activities will be more available if Sue does not have strict times to report to each department and is allowed to manage her own time. Sue might even be able to schedule work in a department when someone she doesn't enjoy seeing is in a meeting, thereby avoiding an unpleasant interaction with a difficult coworker.

No matter what your work arrangements, keeping track of how many days are left before critical dates are reached and seeing that number decline by one each day can improve your mood. Possible dates include your one-year or two-year job anniversary, after which some or all of a signing bonus need not be returned; the length of service point at which a category of benefits becomes available or vests; the time you intend to quit because of a new job, returning to school, or retiring; or the date an employee you particularly dislike is going to leave or transfer to another unit. This suggestion is one example of psychological ways to deal with your job, a topic not discussed in depth here because of so much other literature—on-line and in-print—on gratitude, positivity, and other fruitful ways to think about your job—and life in general.

Chapter Six: If Firing is Imminent

First of all, the good news is that it's very difficult to be fired—absent a major infraction like destroying property, discussing confidential information outside your office, royally screwing up a major project, excessive absence or lateness, insubordination (anything from talking back to your supervisor to refusing to do an assignment), or a remark to or about a person of a sensitive demographic that can be interpreted as racist, sexist, or otherwise offensive to a category of people. More common is a layoff of a group due to a reorganization designed to improve efficiency or as a result of a merger between two firms (including an acquisition of one company by another) where the jobs of similar employees are no longer all necessary.

A major reason why jobs of even relatively poor performers can be secure is the difficulty of replacing employees, especially those who've been on the job for some time with duties not shared by others. Assessing potential new employees means reviewing resumes, phone screenings, and time-consuming interviews by job applicants' potential managers and coworkers. Then it will take some time for a new employee to learn the specific work and to develop necessary relationships with immediate coworkers and those in other departments. Because new hires need time to learn the ropes, they are not typically as valuable as seasoned workers. And there are mistakes in hiring decisions, which is why termination rates within initial probationary periods tend to be high.

A related consideration is the overall state of the economy—especially within your industry. In a recession, it's much easier for employers to find suitable workers than when the economy is booming with plenty of other jobs around and pay raises awarded to induce employees to stay where they are. So not only are your chances of being fired greater in a recession (because of reduced profits) but at those points in the business cycle it's also unfortunately harder to find a new job because of both reduced demand elsewhere and many unemployed competitors for relatively few job vacancies.

Long-term commitments may help avoid—or at least delay—termination. So if it's January and you're working on a project due in March or your company has already paid for you to attend a conference or otherwise travel in April, it will be particularly inefficient or costly to fire you. Sometimes you can volunteer for future events and at the same time signal enthusiasm (which may not really be there) to your supervisor. Maybe an expert in your occupation or industry is visiting your town—or someplace nearby or where a friend or relative of yours lives—to give a talk. Alert your manager about the expert's presentation, and volunteer to attend and take notes that you'll distribute to your coworkers. And don't mention anything about being compensated for travel. You're providing insurance to keep your job longer. Travel expenses pale as compared with the salary you'll be earning prior to and right after you return from the talk—salary you would not have earned if terminated earlier.

Assisting in litigation where your company is being sued is another method of long-term work insurance. You don't have to be a lawyer, just a valuable contributor helping to defend a lawsuit. Suppose the allegation is that your firm has sold faulty products, and your job involves analyzing customer complaints about those products. Demonstrated expertise about the complaints can ensure job security because you may be considered a valuable member of the litigation support team. To enhance your reputation as the complaints expert, from time to time email your in-house lawyers or other prominent officials with such tidbits as: *we received 27 percent of our annual complaints about widgets in February* or *less than one percent of our complaints about gizmos came from customers in California*. Such specialized knowledge suggests you would be very difficult to replace. Because lawyers do not want to compromise their efforts by losing valuable supporting expertise, they may be in-house lobbyists to help you keep your job. And lawsuits can go on for some time.

All this said, if you don't like your work or those you work with, you simply may not have the interest or enthusiasm to achieve a decent performance level. Your heart just isn't in the job. So despite implementing the suggestions in this and the previous chapters, your boss decides you will be terminated. Let's assume this decision is final. What can you do?

The crucial point is not to quit—let them fire you. There are five advantages to waiting to be fired as opposed to quitting. First, you may get severance pay. Second, you may be eligible for unemployment insurance payments. Third, during the time that HR (Human Resources) is preparing your termination, you are still employed and being paid. Fourth, part of your termination package may include help with resume preparation, sessions at job placement organizations, and other activities that can help you network and find a new job—topics on which a great deal is already written. Fifth, there is always the chance that, if you can drag things out enough, something will change and you won't be on the chopping block anymore: obnoxious coworkers—including your boss—may leave your unit (as a result of promotion or transfer) or the firm itself before your termination is finalized; a reorganization will change the employee outlook; or more business will come in and your company can't afford to release even a marginally competent employee like you.

There are two negatives of being fired rather than quitting. First, to a future possible employer, being fired will look worse than having quit—although quitting and then being unemployed awhile does not look good, either. But you may later be able to explain your unemployment—from whatever source—as voluntary downtime out of the labor force when you didn't want a job because of family responsibilities or other issues. And if you were planning to return to school or retire or otherwise take time off, you have no immediate care about finding a new job, anyway. In many cases, should you look for a job in the future, you'll be able to explain your work gap. And prospective employers will generally focus on how your skill set can help them rather than your job history elsewhere.

A second negative is that in order to induce you to quit rather than pay you severance, some managers will try to make your job unpleasant—assigning tasks generally done by lower-level employees; criticizing your work, perhaps even in large meetings; and having someone you don't like or respect go over your recent work with you under the guise of helping you improve. You'll have to remind yourself that it's worth putting up with this treatment for a few extra weeks' pay—and a severance package.

Chapter Seven: Conclusions

Most of the strategies recommended in the previous chapters will not only help you survive your job but will also make you a more productive employee. It's possible that, as a result of following these suggestions, you'll become more interested in your work and gain plaudits from your supervisor—and that should make you hate your job less and maybe even like it! Some ideas, especially those in Chapter Two, are methods of time shifting. They can involve less work but don't need to.

But what about fooling your manager—for example, completing an assignment faster than expected and using the extra time to goof off rather than informing your boss than you're finished and then either doing something on your own that you know your office needs or asking for additional work? Isn't this strategy unethical, contrary to the idea of giving a full day's work for a full day's pay?

First, it's worth noting that only a few of the strategies described earlier fit this category. But more to the point, if you need these occasional breaks to be able to stay at your job and be minimally happy rather than quit or show such dissatisfaction that you'll get fired, then down time like this is maintaining an employer-employee relationship that is beneficial for both parties. Termination is obviously bad for employees and, per the discussion at the beginning of Chapter Six, replacing employees is costly for employers. In addition, suppose in the past you were forced to work late or on the weekend and received no monetary or other appreciation. In that case, the down time you manage to provide for yourself is fair—it counters the extra time worked previously that gave your employer *more* than a full day's work for a full day's pay.

So I make all these recommendations in good conscience. And I hope these suggestions make your work situation less unpleasant—and maybe even turn the corner so you like your job! Good luck!

About the Author

Joseph M. Gilar is retired from a supervisory position at a Fortune 100 company. *How to Survive a Job You Hate* is based on Joe's observations from decades of work.

www.ingramcontent.com/pod-product-compliance
Lightning Source LLC
Chambersburg PA
CBHW071203220526
45468CB00003B/1137